The Puffin Book

by Drew Buckley

Series editor Jane Russ

GRAFFEG

Contents

About This Book

Being a local resident to where these characterful avians call home for a few months of the year, I have spent many years and thousands of hours watching, documenting and photographing puffins at their busiest time of the year, the breeding season, all on this small island off the Pembrokeshire coast, called Skomer.

With a lifelong passion for puffins and through intimate photography, I will take you on a journey through what goes on in the life of a puffin through the breeding season, with insights into their world over the winter months. The book includes details of the puffin's biology, interesting stories and facts I've observed over the years and the trials and tribulations of how the puffin goes about its life.

From the breeding cycle to the habitats and burrows in which they reside, this book will help the reader learn more about what goes on out of view too, as not everything can be captured on camera. There'll be information and facts about what happens both out at sea and underground, especially about the young, which only emerge at their final stages of fledging – a concise presentation of fine photography with life facts and stories for even the hardened puffin fan to enjoy.

This tough little seabird is the epitome of the underdog. Through its characterful face and behaviour it draws you into its world and you're instantly their biggest fan. With their habitats and food sources threatened by climate change and overfishing, it's hoped through this book we can

raise more awareness of the fragile
environment in which they live their
lives and, hopefully, you too will
become a lover of puffins for life.

Skomer Island, Pembrokeshire Coast.

About the Atlantic Puffin

The puffin – such fantastic little birds, they instantly make you smile just looking at them! They're so full of colour and character and even standing still they appear to strike a pose, oozing personality and charm. Sometimes affectionately known as the clowns of the sea or sea parrots, these extremely inquisitive seabirds grace our shores in the springtime, arriving in their thousands to breed. At the same time, they bring joy to many birdwatchers and photographers who head out to the coast to see them.

The puffin, or Atlantic puffin to give it the proper title, belongs to the auk family, a large group of 25 or so species of sea birds all over the world, ranging from razorbills, guillemots and puffins, among others.

Puffins are stocky, plump little birds and are smaller than a lot of people think, compared to their environment or the distances they travel, standing at just 20cm tall, measuring 29cm from the tip of their bill to the tail and weighing about 600g. Their long legs mean they can walk and run quite well on land compared to some other seabirds. The most striking parts of the puffin are undoubtedly their bright orange feet and how can you miss that boldly marked red, orange and grey bill!

Puffins appear to be black and white, but if you look closer you'll notice an array of shades in between, especially around the face. A striking black collar extends around the neck and on the cheeks on each side of the head are areas of grey. These patches meet at the back of the eye and create a crease that leads back to the nape.

The eyes are a light bluish grey in appearance and you can sometimes notice the whites of the eye, a trait which is not too common in the animal kingdom. The eyes are set in a triangular shape, with the vivid orange of the surrounds of the eye most pronounced. The breast and most of the underside are made up of white feathers, leading to orange legs with webbed feet and black claws, which are great for digging.

There's no denying that the puffin's most iconic feature is the bright, colourful beak; this is reserved for the summer months, when it is a lot more obvious and colourful. During the winter, the puffin's beak is quite stubby and dull grey in colour – more like that of a fledgling. Throughout the breeding season, the bill is broad and triangular but quite narrow. The first half of the beak is made up of orangey-red tones with grooved stripes and the rest of the bill is grey in colour. The chevron-shaped lines on the bill can go someway to determining an individual birds' age. A yellow ridge surrounds the bill where it meets the skull and towards the base of the mandibles there is a fleshy bright yellow 'rosette' which aids the puffin's ability to hold fish.

Later in the breeding season, the darker plumage can go more brown than black as they start their transformation into their winter colours. Despite them residing on remote parts of the country through the breeding season, everyone seems to have a universal affinity to the puffin and recognise them even when they have never seen them in the flesh. That could partly be due to their unique colouring and stance. But I like to think it's their sad face that tugs at the heartstrings of the masses and then their small stature, giving them an underdog appearance, and who doesn't root for those guys?

Puffins Through the Seasons

Winter

The Latin name for the Atlantic puffin is *Fratercula arctica*, meaning 'little brother of the Arctic'. This is because the loveable and colourful birds we see in the UK in summer spend most of the winter months out in the colder waters of the northern Atlantic Ocean, where they exist in a life of solitude, dressed in their grey winter colours.

Their breeding grounds cover the coasts of north-west Europe, eastern parts of North America and the Arctic coasts, such as Greenland, Iceland and Scandinavia. The rest of the year Iceland holds over 60 per cent of the world's breeding population of Atlantic puffins, while other large colonies can be found in Newfoundland, the Faroe Islands, the coasts of Norway and the Shetland and Orkney Islands.

Puffins float around the oceans, picking at plankton and fish, but they'll soon need to eat more to have the energy to fly to their breeding grounds. After their winter moult, the birds will boast new flight feathers, which they'll need for frantic feeding and foraging for fish during the summer season that lies ahead. Thick, downy breast feathers, which will help incubate the egg, also start to grow.

On the British mainland you'll find nesting puffins mainly along the coasts that meet the Atlantic, but the main colonies where you can get close-up views are Skomer and Skokholm islands in Pembrokeshire, South Stack on Anglesey, the Farne Islands in the north-east of England, the Isle of May and the Shetland, Bass Rock and Treshnish Isles in Scotland.

These are the most popular for visitors, and as they prefer an island habitat you'll need to take a boat to see them in most cases.

Spring

Shortly before returning to their breeding grounds, puffins need to make an amazing transformation. As the breeding season nears, the dark and dull colours of both sexes are transformed by a hormonal surge within them, resulting in the familiar appearance we know and love.

From a dull winter grey, their feet, beaks and legs all turn vivid orange, standing out against the now dapper white, grey and black feathers. The yellowish rosette at the corner of their mouths enlarges – to help with the upcoming fish deliveries for the chick – and around the rim of the eyes turns into a bright orange colour. All these extravagant and striking changes are expensive for the bird's resources – the vibrant colours come from concentrating large amounts of pigments called carotenoids, which are found widely in the fish they eat. Only if the birds catch plenty of these carotenoid-rich fish will their beaks and legs turn a satisfactory colour. Carotenoids are antioxidants, regulating the metabolism and stimulating the immune system of the fish that contain them as well as the birds that feed on them. Puffins with lots of carotenoids will be better breeders and healthier than those which haven't managed to concentrate the colour, and the colourful puffin in springtime is a signal of its own success, a billboard of health, proving to its peers and its potential mates not only how good it is at fishing, but also at finding the best fish.

This is when we get to see them up close. Older, more mature birds will head for land in the springtime, even to the same colonies where they

were hatched, but they don't just all pile in at once. From spending well over six months at sea, they're quite shy at first and tentative, doing many passes before landing. Even then, they remain extremely wary while on land before taking off again and returning to the safety of the sea. They gather in huge 'rafts', where they pair up with their previous partner to mate.

Considering how well visited puffin colonies are, and how well known puffins are in the animal kingdom,

little is documented about how both sexes pair up. It is understood, however, that after the initial mating takes place the pair return to the same colony every year in a lifelong partnership. As with all seabirds, after the breeding season is over they both go their separate ways until the following spring. Divorce rates in puffins are a lot lower than other species, with scientists observing only around 10 per cent for British birds.

Colony Life

After rafting up, the birds gather and display in a mesmerising fashion, wheeling around and over the colony before settling down for their summer home. The old saying 'first come, first served' reads true, with the early arrivals occupying the more desirable nesting spots, usually where take-off is easiest.

Puffins are quite wary when standing about on land, so there's a definite hierarchy when it comes to nesting – later arrivals are usually pushed towards the extremities of the colony, where they're most at risk of predation. Although they appear quite tame to us, puffins are cautious birds, especially when approaching the colony and looking for a clear space to land.

Again, they're a bit hampered by their wings on landing, with all sorts of final touch downs. Some can pull it off elegantly, whilst some birds come in with a bump and a somersault, shaking themselves off as if nothing happened. It all adds to the character of these comical little birds.

They usually take over old rabbit burrows or excavate their own. The soil on cliff tops is usually quite sandy, making clawing out burrows a breeze.

The inside claws are curved in shape and this adaptation helps them to remove rocks and stones when housekeeping.

Puffins are very energetic when digging and funny to witness as you look on to see the back end of one down a hole with its little feet going, spraying mud and sand skyward and sometimes covering nearby birds! Over time, networks of burrows and tunnels are created, which dries out the top layer of soil in the summer and in turn vastly reduces its structural integrity.

Therefore, it's very important not to walk over burrows at colonies and to stick to any paths, as pressure from above can collapse a chamber quite easily and crush a nesting bird or egg. Colonies are most active and at full capacity in the evenings, with puffins strolling around and standing by their burrows in great numbers.

You'll notice puffins are quite social birds once in and around the colony. They must be, as you can't exactly say the burrows and nesting sites are roomy, and they spend most of their time standing around, interacting with their neighbours and generally watching the world go by. That's not to say they don't bicker with one another, and a lot of pushing and shoving goes on in the colonies, especially over territory.

Puffins are quite dominant when it comes to meeting other birds, sussing each other out and puffing themselves up, standing upright and walking slowly, almost strutting. They move their heads in a jerking fashion and open their beaks, gesturing at one another. If one bird submits, it will lower its head and skulk off, sometimes receiving a quick peck on the rump as it flees.

However, if neither bird backs down, this is when you will witness some scuffling. They grasp each other with their beaks and lock them together, in turn making it more of a wrestling match, trying to push each other backwards and away, sometimes rolling around with wings flapping and feet clawing. I've coined it 'seabird sumo', and it is superb natural behaviour to witness, mostly ending up with one bird retreating and flying off whilst the winning bird stands proud, stretching and flapping its wings in an almost celebratory pose, but more than likely putting the ruffled feathers back into place!

I've even witnessed two birds, neither backing down, rolling together in a ball off the cliffs and down the ledges, separating in mid-air and landing in the ocean, dazed and confused.

They're also very vocal in and around the colony, making purring noises to one another, whether it be bonding with a mate or gesturing to passers-by; there's not much variation in their vocabulary though, with their general groaning sound akin to a miniature chainsaw.

When not flying around or down in the burrow, you'll spot puffins just standing around or perching on rocks. This also runs true for a lot of the non-breeding birds as well, who have even less to do. You'll notice birds sleeping during the day, waking every few minutes to check the coast is clear. They're mainly inactive at night too, but how much sleep they have per day is still a bit of a mystery.

Puffins spend a lot of time preening and setting their feathers into the correct position with their claws or beaks. Especially for a seabird, caring for their feathers is a necessity, and if you've ever watched puffins, you'll know it's very time-consuming.

Usually, the first thing they do when returning to the colony is to make sure they're in tip-top condition. Unique barbs on the feathers lock together for waterproofness while diving and puffins regularly reshape them.

Their feathers are made up of hundreds of small branches that need to be kept in their tracts too, and preening and shaking can help settle any out-of-line feathers. I've watched plenty of birds using their feet and claws to scratch hard-to-reach places, but it seems with little effort the puffin can reach almost any feather on its body.

They spend much of the day preening and keeping their feathers and plumage in good order. They do this using their beak and by spreading preen oil from their uropygial gland, located at the base of the tail. Preen oil helps condition and protect the feathers with a mixture of antibiotics, fatty acids, wax and substances reactive to vitamin D from sunlight.

Swimming

Even though we see them pottering about on land, puffins are seabirds, after all. Out at sea they tend to lead a solitary lifestyle and are quite comical when spotted alongside a boat. They bob about, pushing themselves forward using their strong legs and large webbed feet. Like most seabirds, they always try to face into the wind, even when they're resting, and stay afloat thanks to their unique feathers. The outer feathers act as a life jacket, thanks to their tiny barbs and hooked barbules. These lock together, making the feathers almost airtight, helping create buoyancy and keeping them warm in inclement weather.

Puffins spend most of their lives paddling on the open waves – it's only through the breeding season they're confined more to their colonies.

They dive little and often for food, sometimes reaching extremes of 60 metres, but they generally find food between around 5 and 30 metres, with their dives lasting 10 or 20 seconds.

You'll notice with most seabirds there's not a lot of colour to their bodies, with the majority being black on top and white underneath. I'd like to think this is camouflage from aerial predators when they're out at sea, as it's hard to spot something dark on dark water from above. On the flip side, anything coming up from underneath should have a hard time spotting a white object against the bright sky.

Like other seabirds that reside on the water's surface, their take-off is a spectacle too. They thrust themselves forward with their feet,

pattering and skipping across the water whilst flapping their wings to gain enough lift to head skywards. Sometimes waves can hamper progress, resulting in a crash or belly flop. Puffins are sturdy characters though, so in not too much time they're airborne again.

Whilst the puffin appears to struggle to stay airborne with its very rapid wing beats, underwater they move capably, extending their wings and paddling with sharp, thrusting pushes whilst using their feet as a rudder. Puffins are able to swim quite fast underwater and can hold their breath for up to a minute.

Flying

Due to their colour, shape and behaviour, puffins and other auks are often described as 'flying penguins'. Although these species aren't related and reside in separate hemispheres, the two families do share very similar characteristics and traits: both are black and white with coloured beaks, both mainly eat a fish diet, both dive for food and 'fly' through the water using their wings, both are accustomed to colder waters and breed in bustling colonies. Their shared characteristics are evidence of the adaptations species make to survive in similar environments.

When in flight they're like little torpedoes, with their wings beating furiously to stay airborne and making the viewer wonder whether they are made for flying at all.

The size of the wing in relation to the body is quite small, which is a compromise between flight functionality and underwater performance.

In full flight, it's known that puffins can reach speeds of over 60mph and flap their wings at nearly 600 beats per minute, impressive statistics for such a small seabird. The constant need for fast wing beats is to counteract the risk of stalling, so to save energy the birds use the wind to their advantage. With updrafts and gusts common on cliff faces, it's easy to watch a puffin flying effortlessly at the colonies.

On excessively blustery days, I've watched many puffins land by backing into the wind and then hover in the air on take-off, making them look very at home with their wings.

Through the aid of photography and high-speed continuous sequences, we can break down the approach for landing: the birds enter a glide stage before putting their wings forward to slow them down, the wingtips

bending with the force as they enter a stall and a fast flap to control the descent. They sometimes use their feet as air brakes and their tails as a rudder.

They're fascinating to watch as they come streaming in one by one into the colony. This is, of course, totally dependent on the wind direction and overshoots are common, requiring another lap of the colony before they can touch down.

Summer

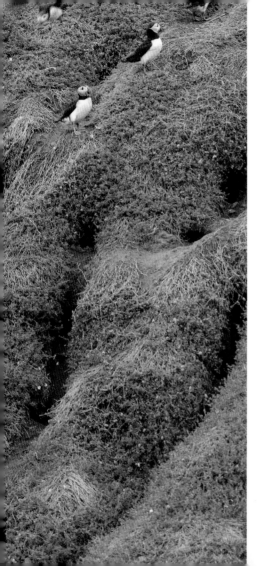

Burrows and Breeding

The main reason puffins return to land in the spring months is to breed. Spending most of the winter out on the ocean, they meet up with their life partner on the way back to the breeding colony. Many other auks, such as guillemots and razorbills, will pack tightly in their breeding colonies and lay their eggs on the bare rock, uncovered, and out in the open on cliff edges – a very precarious process. Puffins, however, prefer some home comforts and use burrows, meaning there is some excavating to do before they can enjoy the benefits of a dry chamber through the breeding season. Some couples will return to the same burrow early every year and fiercely defend it against prospective intruders.

On Skomer, for instance, a lot of the work has been done already by old rabbit burrows, which can be taken over. These require some slight adjustments and housekeeping, such as enlarging the tunnel chambers and clearing out old grass and stones, sometimes over their partner standing outside!

For later arrivals or many first-time breeding birds who need to create a new burrow, it's a case of getting down to the task of moving a large amount of earth for a small bird. New burrows take a few weeks to create, with both birds digging for a couple of hours per day, and when they're not digging they're defending the site from any neighbours who want to hijack their hard work.

On Skomer, near the cliff edges, where the burrows are very dusty and old and holding little grass above, many burrow chambers interlink in a labyrinth of tunnels and balconies. Generally, puffin burrows are around a metre long, in some instances up to two metres, but it's hard to imagine a seabird like a puffin walking underground: a cramped tunnel, just big enough for itself, digging away in the dark and then carrying fish to its chick at the end of this black hole – extraordinary birds!

Chicks are born with a real aversion to light for their own safety until they fledge, so it's important that the tunnel is dark through daylight hours.

Depending on the location of the colony, the nesting possibilities on offer vary. Skomer mostly has plenty of soil and vegetation, however, at other colonies where only rocks and ledges are present, birds will occupy all sorts of cracks, gaps and rocky crevices in pursuit of a nesting site out of the weather. While it may be comfier and safer in your burrow, constructing them is no mean feat.

Like when mammals, such as badgers, create a sett, digging into a slope is a lot easier and allows for a stronger structure than digging down into flat ground. One issue with flat ground is that the ceiling of the burrow chamber can become worn and incredibly thin. The soil can also dry out quickly, which in turn kills off the vegetation that holds the soil together, overall resulting in a very weak roof, especially if pressure is applied from above by the walking of humans or livestock. On flatter land at the colonies, it's not uncommon for the ground to have humps on it where vegetation grows or previous excavation heaps; these are what puffins aim for when starting a burrow.

The burrows themselves are quite narrow, just big enough for the puffin to walk through while bent forwards. They're around 15cm in diameter and end in the nesting chamber, where the egg is laid. They also create a side chamber for the chick to defecate in, keeping the chamber itself clean. Once the nesting chamber is dug, then it's time to furnish it, ready for egg laying. They start out by collecting and carrying bits of grass, twigs or plant roots for the nest, sometimes passing the offerings to their partners to strengthen the mutual bond between them. This is then taken underground to line the nest.

It's amazing watching this process.
Sometimes they'll just pick up a
small stone and walk around with
it for a few minutes, then drop that
and pluck some flowers and almost
play with them, picking up and
dropping things as they go; they're
so inquisitive and extremely curious,
finding the right pieces to take down
the burrow.

You'll also notice plenty of signs of affection and the behaviour of 'billing'. This is where the pair of birds approach each other, shaking their heads from side to side and rattling their bills together once up close. It's an important aspect in the courtship ritual of the puffin, occurring many times throughout the breeding season to affirm the bond.

Eggs and Early Days

Depending on the colony's latitude, egg laying starts in April for the majority and the female lays just one egg each year. However, if this is lost or predated, research has shown they can sometimes lay another before the season is out. Like most birds, puffins have feather-free brood patches on either side of their bodies to conduct heat to the egg and keep it warm. Their eggs are much larger than chicken eggs by comparison (about 6cm long), considering the size difference of the birds, and are white in colour. Once the egg has been laid, both parents take it in turns to incubate it over the course of five to seven weeks. They must time it right to coincide with the fish stocks arriving.

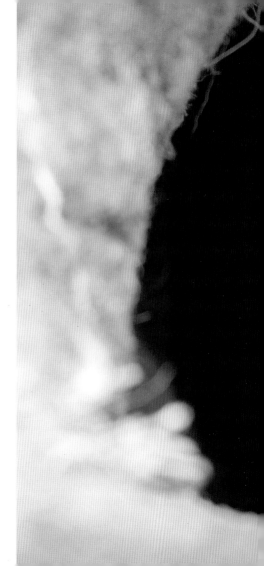

With current climate change and sea temperatures fluctuating, which in turn alter the transit patterns of fish, it's been reported that some seabird and puffin colonies completely fail to raise any young, due to there being no food sources available.

When incubating, the parent frequently takes breaks, sometimes even flying out to sea for a short swim and wash before returning and placing the egg under one of the brood patches, holding it in place with its wing.

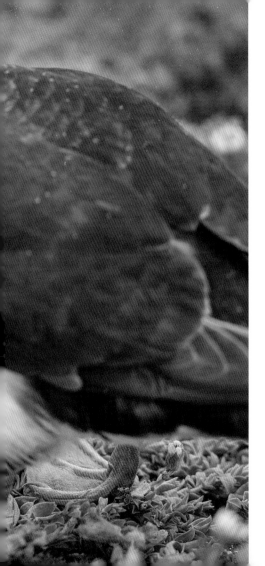

On hatching, the puffin chick is well developed, far more developed than a garden bird chick, for instance. The new-born 'puffling' is covered in soft black down over most of its body, other than the whitish colour of its chest and underparts. The chick's eyes open shortly after hatching and they are soon dry and fully aware of their surroundings in the burrow. The parents will still sit on the chick over the next week to keep it warm before it can start to regulate temperature for itself. They're quite tough little guys at this stage and can be left on their own while the parents head out to forage for food, although the chick will remain in the burrow and dependent on the parents bringing in fish until it fledges.

Feeding

When visiting a colony, the parents
visibly bringing fish back to the nests
indicates that chicks have been born.
Early in the chick's life, the parents
pass the fish to them underground,
but as the chick grows older the
parent birds drop the fish into the
burrow, allowing the chick to feed
itself.

The classic shot of the puffin is with a mouthful of sandeels, so there's no surprise to anyone that their diet consists mainly of fish. Puffins are amazing hunters, 'flying' through the water using their strong wings as paddles. The bird chases its prey at speed through the shoals, reaching substantial depths and staying underwater for up to a minute.

Before diving, they must let the air out of those locked feathers. Muscles under the skin allow the bird to flatten and force the air out of them, enabling them to dive unhindered. They can consume larger fish, around seven inches long, but most of the time their chosen food are sandeels, sprats, herring and capelin – they need to consume around 40 of these per day. Researchers have studied the puffin's feeding habits and noticed they also occasionally eat shrimp, molluscs, marine worms and other crustaceans when fish aren't so abundant. They can swallow fish whole underwater, but most of the time they bring them up to the surface or return to the burrow to eat.

As you may have noticed with puffins, they can cram loads of fish into one mouthful. They cruise through the water, scooping up the fish one by one and moving them to the back of their mouths using the grooved tongue like a conveyor belt. Here they can hold them in place whilst they catch some more.

The two mandibles (upper and lower parts of the beak) are hinged uniquely and can be held parallel to one another, allowing the puffin to hoard a row of fish in place. At the same time, the fish are kept secure by inward-facing serrations and spines inside the upper mandible. The average catch for a beak full of sandeels is usually around 10, with record numbers topping over 60 fish. I would imagine this record-breaking catch was made up of smaller fish though, as sandeels are quite large.

Another interesting feature of the beak is the nostrils. As you can imagine, when catching fish underwater you're going to consume some seawater each time and surviving at sea without fresh water is a big problem for many species, puffins included. So how do they cope? Puffins have specially adapted nostrils that are located at either side of the upper beak, which not only allow the bird to breathe but also contain salt-draining glands near the eye. Puffins and other seabirds have these glands to extract salt-filled fluid from their bloodstream – the extracted liquid is five times saltier than the bird's own blood. This densely salty fluid is ejected through the nostrils and runs down grooves in the beak in drops. As the drops get larger, you'll notice the birds shaking their heads, sending the salt back to the sea.

Adult Life, Predators and Threats

Puffins, unlike many other bird species, have a reasonably long life expectancy. To think that birds I see born on Skomer every year can live for 20 years on average is amazing. Some puffins have even been recorded at reaching 40 years old, and with the fledging survival rate at over 90 per cent they're a tough and successful species!

They certainly don't have an easy life though, not only contending with the weather fronts the Atlantic Ocean produces but also being bullied by gulls and skuas, especially when taking fish back to their burrows. When on land at their breeding colonies is the most dangerous time for predation.

Ground predators, such as rats, are the most documented problem at seabird colonies and can decimate eggs and chicks in their burrows. Puffins generally choose to nest on islands and the more remote parts of the mainland ground-based predators cannot access. There is, however, a lot of danger from the sky, especially when coming back to their burrows with fish.

Many birds predate puffins, skuas and the great and lesser black-backed gulls, among others, who wait around to mob an incoming puffin of its fish supper. The hunting grounds for puffins are usually quite some way away from the colony, with birds travelling up to 60 miles or more to reach the fishing grounds.

This commute for food starts to attract unwanted attention. On returning with a mouthful of fish, the puffins run the gauntlet through the awaiting gulls. Skuas and great black-backed gulls are massive in size and weight compared to a puffin and are an absolute menace during the breeding season. These fish pirates regularly chase incoming puffins in the hope they'll drop the fish. Worse, they even sometimes grab them in flight until they yield their bounty.

Most of the time the gulls will patrol the nesting sites on foot, in the hope of intercepting an incoming puffin with fish. In some cases, I've watched gulls heading down the entrance of a burrow after a puffin – the panic on the innocent puffin's face is clear to see. I've even seen mobbed puffins head down their neighbour's burrow out of harm's way of an attacking gull!

The way the larger predators mainly feed is called kleptoparasitism, which is the process of harassing another bird until they give up their food. Puffins have learnt to partly counteract this by all flying in at the same time, the adage of safety in numbers, almost baffling the gulls by having too many puffins to choose from.

It isn't just the fish the gull is after – they are more than capable of taking an unsuspecting puffin (or puffling!) too and devouring it, especially some great skuas, which will actively hunt

adult puffins. However, it's mainly the fish they tend to go for and most puffins give up their catch without any contact being needed. Puffins are very alert at all times and if startled by a passing gull or bird of prey you'll find groups of them suddenly take off and head down to the reasonable safety of the sea before doing a few circuits of the colony and returning when it's safe.

Another danger to puffins and puffin populations is the sea itself. As puffins mainly spend the winter out on the ocean, they can drown by being caught up in the surf and swell, with hurricane-force winds whipping up the waves. In recent years, violent winter storms have caused seabirds to fall foul of the harsh conditions. The aftermath of this is hundreds of seabirds, known as wrecks, washing up on the shores. Birds involved in these incidents mainly die through starvation, becoming emaciated and unable to feed near the surface due to the large waves and strong currents.

These are severe circumstances though and most of the time the majority make it through. Population numbers are counted during the breeding season, with the UK holding nearly 600,000 pairs.

Overall, species numbers are decreasing, but not enough to warrant concern on an international threatened species status list. Some put the decline down to an increased number of predatory birds, the introduction of rats and cats onto some of the islands they colonise and also marine pollution and hazards, such as drowning in fishing nets, toxic contamination, oil spills or the reduction in fish stocks due to climate change. Some colonies have decreased vastly while others are on the increase.

On Lundy (which means 'puffin island' in Norse), for instance, populations decreased from 3500 pairs to just 10 pairs in the year 2000, attributed to the introduction of rats to the island. Since the eradication of the rats, puffin populations are now increasing once more.

On the outer reaches of the UK, populations have been steadily rising on islands such as Skomer, the Isle of May and the Farne Islands at about 10 per cent a year. British populations are minor in comparison to the five million-plus colonies of Iceland and North America, but it's good to see there's still a stronghold on our shores. As cute as they appear, they're still a staple diet for some countries around the world, and not too long ago this included offshore British islands such as the Faroes and St. Kilda. It must have been quite a spectacle back then to see men, women and children descending the cliffs to collect puffins for their dinner using nets and poles with no form of safety ropes. To this day, they are served up as a speciality in some Icelandic restaurants, however, in most countries the Atlantic puffin is now protected by legislation and where hunting is still allowed there are strict laws and limits on the amount people can catch.

Fledging

Young birds are nicknamed pufflings. They're dull in colour with grey faces and beaks and extremely fluffy – not to mention cute – in the early weeks. A puffling takes four to seven weeks to fledge and at the later stages it will make the odd appearance at the edge of the burrow, coming out to exercise its wings, defecate and take in the sea air. They still have some aversion to light and seem to avoid being right in the open. At the burrow entrance, pufflings are constantly checking for danger and are very wary, ducking back into the safety of the burrow with anything that moves or flies overhead.

While growing up, the chicks' inquisitive nature sees them wandering around the burrow, playing with nesting material or pecking at scuttling invertebrates.

At this stage, they're incredibly battle born, attacking any intruders. Research has shown that you can swap chicks between burrows and the adult will still feed them, suggesting that the parents don't recognise their chick by sight or sound but will generously feed any youngster in their burrow.

Near the time of fledging, daytime onlookers will witness the puffling at the burrow entrance, fiercely guarded by the adult, while it exercises its fully feathered wings rapidly, readying for the upcoming leap of faith. This could be in a few days, or it could be that night, but only when the puffling is ready will it leave.

At around 70 per cent of the adult's weight and equipped with strong wings, it makes its way to the cliff edge and takes the plunge. Most seabird chicks, such as guillemots and razorbills, aren't as developed at fledging and go through a more daredevil approach, sometimes bouncing on the way down to the sea. With other auks, the chicks swim out to sea with their father, and due to the fact they fledged at a less-developed stage they still depend on their parent for food somewhat. Puffin chicks, though, fledge later as a bigger and stronger bird, and with more fat reserves they are prepared to take on the world and ready to fight for themselves.

Chicks leave the burrow under the cover of darkness, when the risk of predation is low, unseen and unshepherded by their parents, who will remain at the colony for many days after the chick has left. Sometimes the adults will be seen bringing food back to the burrow, dropping it by the entrance only for it to remain uneaten – a cue for the parents to cease providing for their young. The chicks will now be on their own out in the ocean with no more contact from their parents, not returning to land for another two or three years and turning four or five years old before finding a mate.

The parents breathe a sigh of relief and head out to sea to begin their solitary transformation, in reverse, as it were, from their orange-accented summer splendour to their dull grey winter plumage. The now shortening late summer days trigger a decrease in their sexual hormones, and with the shrinking of their reproductive and egg-laying organs their colours begin to fade. Once at sea, even their impressive bills and facial patches will drop away. It's an amazing transformation, but there's no point incurring the costs of being this colourful when there is no more breeding to be done. The birds are essentially turning back the clock to a time before puberty, losing their sexuality and adulthood with its burdens and responsibilities to focus on their own survival.

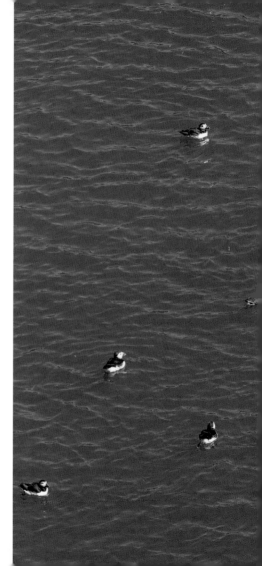

Autumn

The Great Migration

About 90 per cent of all puffins return year on year to their burrows, which is an amazing success rate. Until recently, no one knew where they went or how the birds returned to the colonies. It was assumed the puffins scattered into the wide-open oceans, with the first hint of springtime sunshine stirring their genetic transformation and their desire to mate, but recent tracking experiments run by an expert team from Oxford University, led by bird migration specialist Tim Guildford, have brought to light what was previously a mystery.

On Skomer Island, Pembrokeshire, 27 individual birds were tagged with geolocators to record where the puffins had been over the entire winter by measuring the times each day at dawn and dusk. Stored light level measurements can be used to derive dawn and dusk transition times, from which it is possible to estimate an approximate location anywhere on earth (except during periods of a few weeks around the equinoxes). These geolocators were then retrieved the following spring on Skomer, and with the data downloaded the birds were refitted with the trackers for the following winter. Between 2007-2010, the team gathered nearly 50 bird-years of data. The results are mind-boggling and an amazing insight into the puffins' lives through the winter.

Each puffin in the study seemed to follow a different route, confirming along with previous sightings at sea that puffins winter alone.

Dispersive Migration in the Atlantic Puffin

Patterns of migratory movements for 18 puffins tracked using geolocators are shown as median individual position estimates during three months outside the breeding season.

⬤ August

⬤ October

⬤ February

Lines join each individual bird's successive positions, but do not indicate the path travelled.

From Guilford T, Freeman R, Boyle D, Dean B, Kirk H, Phillips R, et al. (2011) *A Dispersive Migration in the Atlantic Puffin and Its Implications for Migratory Navigation*. PLoS ONE 6(7): e21336. https://doi.org/10.1371/journal.pone.0021336

Plotting the yearly data on a map revealed some extraordinary behaviour, with each bird repeating a very consistent and complex series of routes unique to itself, year after year.

For instance, in 2008-2009 the puffin named EJ47617 left the isthmus on Skomer and headed north-west to the waters south of Iceland for the autumn before travelling south a huge distance to overwinter in the Mediterranean and finally returning to Skomer in the spring. It repeated this same route, albeit slightly different, the following year. The maps show the birds going overland, a result from the rough co-ordinates generated by the geolocations, but it is more probable the birds would always fly across the relative safety of water, where they can bathe and feed.

Another bird in the study, EJ09593, started in similar fashion, heading north-west, but went on to spend autumn in the waters below Greenland. It headed east, near to Iceland, over Christmas and the New Year before descending south to the west of Ireland for the winter, then finally returning to Skomer, covering a near identical route the following year.

EJ99427 seems to prefer the waters of Great Britain, not venturing too far away, with the Faroe Islands its most northern point and the Bay of Biscay to its southern reaches. Of course, the weather, sea conditions and food sources will ultimately dictate where the birds venture, so there's always some variation in the migration routes, but you can pretty much predict where a puffin will likely go in the upcoming winter, and that's wherever it went last year!

Individual Birds Migration Map

Migratory tracks of eight individual puffins in two successive years.
Each individual is indicated in a different colour and position estimates are given as monthly medians of available data, with the month indicated by a number (January – 1).

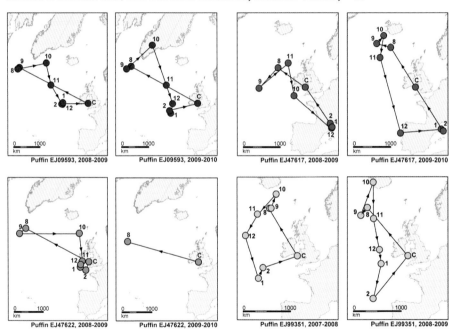

Puffin EJ09593, 2008-2009

Puffin EJ09593, 2009-2010

Puffin EJ47617, 2008-2009

Puffin EJ47617, 2009-2010

Puffin EJ47622, 2008-2009

Puffin EJ47622, 2009-2010

Puffin EJ99351, 2007-2008

Puffin EJ99351, 2008-2009

From Guilford T, Freeman R, Boyle D, Dean B, Kirk H, Phillips R, et al. (2011) *A Dispersive Migration in the Atlantic Puffin and Its Implications for Migratory Navigation.* PLoS ONE 6(7): e21336. https://doi.org/10.1371/journal.pone.0021336

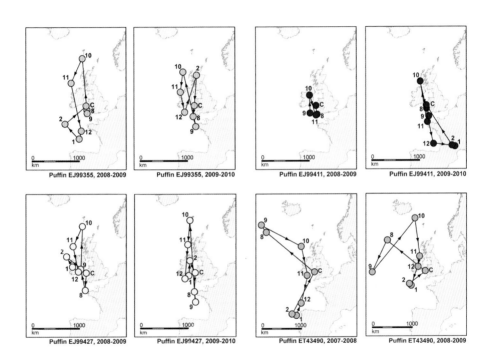

Puffin EJ99355, 2008-2009

Puffin EJ99355, 2009-2010

Puffin EJ99411, 2008-2009

Puffin EJ99411, 2009-2010

Puffin EJ99427, 2008-2009

Puffin EJ99427, 2009-2010

Puffin ET43490, 2007-2008

Puffin ET43490, 2008-2009

They will undoubtedly come across one another out on the open waves, but their actions in migratory terms are based on their own destiny and, if any, their previous experiences, rather than that of their parents or others. It's thought that many young puffins head out on random tracks, exploring the world for themselves and learning the ocean as they go. Some don't venture far, while some cover millions of square miles. Many find refuge in the food sources of the Mid-Atlantic Ridge and some head south and east into the Mediterranean. Ultimately, it goes without question that those birds who find a good food source will survive and those that don't will never breed. This information, learned as young birds, becomes fixed in a puffin's mind and it's this mental map of waypoints that they rely on, year in, year out.

They are very much individuals, leading extraordinary lives, through the perils of the breeding season to the sea storms that rage in the Atlantic Ocean, transforming between the vibrant, hormone-driven colours of their summer splendour to their solitary, drop-in-the-ocean existence of a monotone winter. Two differing existences, two differing birds, both sides not more important than the other, and both of which depend on the survival of the species.

Next time you sit among the puffins on a spring day or summer evening, staring at their quizzical faces and enjoying their exceptional aesthetic beauty, bear a thought for not only their current yearly life cycles but what the puffin stands for as a species – not just clowns of the sea but heroes of the ocean, Ice Age survivors and Atlantic conquerors, their minds constantly thinking ahead, swinging between life at land or sea, swimming alone or raising young, exploring the waves or digging burrows, the never-ending fluctuations of life as a puffin.

Questions & Answers

Q – How many species of puffin are there in the world?

A – Four: Atlantic, horned, tufted and rhinoceros.

Q - Puffins are well known for holding many fish in their beaks, but what is the most fish that a puffin has ever been seen holding at once?

A – 62.

Q - Atlantic puffins are renowned for their large, colourful beaks, but what recent discovery by a Nottingham University student makes them even more amazing?

A - Their beaks glow under UV light. No one is sure why yet, but it could be used to attract a mate.

Q - After a winter at sea, Atlantic puffins return to the same burrow with the same mate, year after year. Once reunited, both puffins affectionately knock beaks in a display known as what?

A – Billing.

Q - Puffins are not known for their aerial abilities, but they are remarkable flyers. How many times a minute are they able to flap their wings?

A – 400 times.

Q - How did puffins get their name?

A – The word puffin is thought to be derived from the word 'puff', which refers to swollen or puffed up.

Q – How do returning adult birds find their partners in the seabird colony?

A – By smell.

Q - Which island, located in the Bristol Channel, takes its name

from the old Norse word for puffin?

A – Lundy Island. *Lundi* is the Old Norse word for puffin – though it might also refer to a copse or wooded area.

Q - How long are puffin eggs incubated for?

A – 36 to 45 days.

Q - When is the only time puffins spend time on land?

A – When they are nesting.

Q - What is the collective noun for a group of puffins?

A – There are various names, but my favourite is 'circus'. With their colourful beaks, they are truly the clowns of the sea.

Q – What do puffins eat?

A - A selection of fish, but sandeels are their favourite.

Q - What is a puffin's drink of choice?

A – Water. They can drink salty seawater direct from the oceans and expel the excess salt out of the glands in their nostrils.

Q - How do puffins manage to stack fill their beaks with food?

A – They have unique straight-opening beaks, a tongue that works like a conveyor belt, pushing fish to the back of their mouths, and also backward-facing barbs in the top part of their mouth that hold all the fish in place.

Q - Does any country have the puffin as its national bird? If so, which?

A - The Atlantic puffin is the official bird symbol of the province of Newfoundland and Labrador, Canada.

Q – How many puffins breed on Skomer and Skokholm?

A – Total numbers vary year on year, but the five-year trend is increasing, with over 30,000 birds between the two islands.

Myth, Legends and Art

by Jane Russ

Faroe Islands

In the Faroe Islands (situated in the seas north of Scotland and between Iceland and Norway), puffins are called *prestur* or priests. This is understandable if you have ever seen puffins walking on land, leaning forward slightly, almost appearing to have their arms behind their backs. The genus name of the puffin is *Fratercula,* which includes the Latin word for brother, *frater*. This can, of course, also be interpreted as friar or 'little brother'. Furthermore, they hold their feet together when taking to the air, which could be interpreted as 'praying hands'.

Ireland

Irish Celtic folklore has them as the reincarnation of monks, which may account for the fact that, generally, the Irish would not eat them, in spite of their profusion during the breeding season. The exception to this was on the Blasket Islands off County Kerry. In 1953, by which time there were only 28 inhabitants left on the islands, they were abandoned as being unsustainable. However, once on the mainland, these remaining islanders, who had dwelt in a close-knit Irish-speaking community, were encouraged to write about and record what life had been like in such an inhospitable place.

Maurice O'Sullivan, who was born in 1904 on Great Blasket, lived there until 1927. In his island memoir *Twenty Years A-Growing* (1933) he

PLATE CCXIII

Drawn from Nature by J.J. Audubon F.R.S. F.L.S.

Engraved, Printed & Coloured by R. Havell 1834

Puffin. MORMON ARCTICUS. *1.Male. 2. Female.*

explains how he would catch and kill up to three dozen 'whipeens' (young puffins). Between the mid-1930s and the mid-1950s, the drop in the number of islanders meant that food was often at close to starvation levels, and, consequently, the numbers of birds dropped because of overhunting. In his book *The Birds of the Blasket Islands* (1954), S. M. D. Alexander estimated there to be only four to six pairs on Great Blasket, whereas a recent visitor wrote, 'The puffins were so numerous, they seemed almost like insects swarming through the air.'

Another pair of islands off the County Kerry coast with a large puffin colony are the Skellig Islands. Comprising two rocky outcrops, Skellig Michael and Little Skellig, they are responsible for a 'modern legend' of worldwide proportions.

The makers of *Star Wars: The Last Jedi* were looking for a location with some ancient dwellings to act as the place Luke Skywalker would have gone to hone his Jedi skills, and the Skelligs were perfect in one respect in that Skellig Michael had been home to monks in an early Christian monastery since at least the 8th century and had wonderful and very photogenic winding steps, buildings and monastic cells. The one snag was that it was the protected site for hundreds of puffins and the filmmakers wanted to shoot in the breeding season.

They were allowed to shoot on condition that the birds were not disturbed, and so a new *Star Wars* animated animal was born through the wonders of CGI, the porg. With hundreds of birds moving and flocking around, it was decided by

FRATERCULA ARCTICA LIN. $^5/_{10}$
Lunnefågel.

Wall art by Aspire at Leake Street, London, 2020, highlighting Birds of Conservation Concern and the International Union for Conservation of Nature red lists of declining or endangered species.

the production and design teams that it would be far too costly to edit the birds out, so they would create an animal rather like a puffin that was indigenous to the island.

Scotland

A tammie norie, the name for the puffin in Shetland and the northern islands, is first referenced in Robert Chambers's *The Popular Rhymes of Scotland* (1870): 'Tammie Norie o' the Bass, Canna kiss a bonny lass.' This is said jocularly when a young man refuses to salute a rustic coquette. The puffin, which builds in great numbers on the Bass Rock, is a very shy bird with a long deep bill, giving him an air of stupidity, and from these two things together the saying has probably arisen. It is also customary to call a stupid-looking man a tammie norie.

Cornwall

It is believed in Cornish mythology that King Arthur reincarnated as a puffin and visits the favourite haunts of his life in this guise. The raven is also credited with this reincarnation.

Iceland

From the 13th century, the Icelandic book the *Snorra Edda* has a reference to puffins. The Icelandic word for puffin is *lundi* and they are credited with being able to predict storms and bad weather of all types. Any sensible puffin would make its way to land two or three days before a storm, and this drive for self-preservation led Icelanders to the belief that puffins flocking to land is an indication that hatches should be battened down.

Furthermore, flocking birds diving out at sea is an indicator of shoals of fish.

Raw puffin heart was traditionally eaten as a culinary treat in Iceland, however, it has fallen out of favour in more recent times. To make puffin meat more palatable, it is soaked in brine, smoked, boiled, chilled and then served cold. The Thjodhatid Festival (people's feast) has been held in July at Vestmannaeyjar on one of the Westman Islands off Iceland's south coast since 1874. Smoked puffin, along with other tasty snacks, is still served to the festivalgoers from a village of over 300 tents. Puffin was a staple of the festival in the past, but these days it has been superseded by more usual burgers and chicken dippers. Interestingly, although puffins are not endangered and Iceland has the largest population, estimated at somewhere between 7 and 10 million, their numbers are declining. This is because, although they live up to 30 years, their usual lifespan is about 16 years, and they are creatures of habit.

Right: The Thjodhatid Festival, Iceland.

Puffin mural, Seward, Alaska.

They come back to the same nest-hole and the same partner every year, which is perfect, until global warming lets mackerel move further north and decimate the sand eel population, which is the puffin's staple food. While the sandeels move to shoal in new places, the puffins still go to the original fishing grounds. The puffins in Iceland are still coming back, but they are older birds and not laying eggs because their food sources are diminishing. It is not illegal to hunt puffin after the breeding season in July in Iceland or the Faroe Islands.

Inuit Culture

Some Inuit societies are known to make a musical instrument from collected puffin bills, and the shaker produced is thought to have power to heal the sick. It is also believed amongst Inuits that puffins can alter the weather and stop the creation of storms.

There is a Native American puffin myth which starts with an Atlantic puffin and ends with a tufted puffin:

There was a young woman of a coast-dwelling tribe who, every time she passed a small island in her father's canoe would say, 'I wish I could sit among those birds, they are so pretty.' Some time later, whilst looking for a place to land on the island with other young women, the canoe they are in is overturned by a wave and they all drown. All, that is, except the heroine, who is taken in and saved by the birds, having heard her saying how beautiful she thought they were.

A death feast is held in the village, as it is thought that all had drowned in the accident. However, a short while later, her father is out in his canoe fishing with others when someone shouts that he sees his daughter up on the cliff with the birds.

The father, who is rich, tries to offer gifts of animal pelts to the birds in exchange for his daughter, but to no avail. Nonetheless, her mother has an idea. The girl's mother still has the white hair of her own grandfather stored in a box and suggests that it might make a better bargaining tool for the birds. On the mother's instruction, they put boards across the canoes, spread the hair out and paddle out to the island.

When they reach the island, they can see the girl sitting on the cliff. All the birds fly down, take a tuft of white hair and attach it to their own heads, but the girl does not move. The tufted puffins speak to their chief and suggest that this is a fair exchange. The chief agrees, but not before he tells the girl that she would be welcome to return to the island any time that she is tired of human company.

Tufted puffins sculpture, Cannon Beach, Oregon.

The Lundy Rabbit's Complaint
by Dru Marland

Who's this odd bloke puffed up there outside my hole?
I only nipped out for some dandelion, and when I got back
There he was, bold as you like in his black dinner jacket,
Saying, "Come in here dressed like that? That won't do at all!"

The cheek of it!
We came over with the Normans,
I'll have you know.
In fact, my people have often dined with royalty.
And now here's this blow-in, shirt still wet from the sea.
Maybe he's drunk?
He's got a nose on him like a rainbow.
Ouch.
Nasty nip to it too.

Says they're only here for the summer season
And then they'll be off cruising down to Spain, when the puffling's
Gone away to college.
Empty nesters eh, he said, feathers ruffling
Not empty enough if you ask me, thought I, with reason,
Thinking of the kits' old nest down there, my belly fur and hay,
And the pong of fishbones and guano that'll never go away.

Drew Buckley

Drew is an award-winning professional landscape and wildlife photographer based in Pembrokeshire, south-west Wales. Drew's talents cover landscape,

wildlife and astro photography, photojournalism and all aspects of commercial photography. Inspired by his brothers, he picked up a camera at a young age and got a 35mm film Canon SLR back in the late 90s. After a career as a computer games 3D artist, he became a full-time professional photographer in 2010. Since then he's authored three books: the photo and visitor location guidebook *Photographing South Wales,* published by FotoVue, and two titles, *Puffins*, a pocket book, and the photography for *Wilder Wales*, published by Graffeg, who also publish his range of calendars every year.

His work has been featured in countless magazines, such as *BBC Countryfile*, *BBC Wildlife*, *Outdoor Photography*, *Digital SLR*, *Photo Plus*,

The Great Outdoors and Country Walking, and national newspapers such as The Times and the Guardian. Drew regularly takes on photography commissions. His clients include Pembrokeshire Coast National Park, National Trust, Natural Resources Wales, RSPB, Wildlife Trust, NHS Wales and many south Wales businesses and organisations. He was also involved in producing many of the time-lapse sequences and seasonal transitions showcased in The Pembrokeshire Coast: A Wild Year, a UK-wide BBC Natural History programme shot over two years, featuring his home county of Pembrokeshire.

Drew is an ambassador for LEE Filters, who support his landscape photography workshops for all abilities, and he is also an official Wildlife Trust commercial operator permitted to run day and overnight courses on Skomer Island. His commercial work also includes time-lapse photography, covering events and marketing, having recently expanded into video production.

Drew has gained many awards and commendations in UK and worldwide photography competitions over the past ten years. He's featured in the British Wildlife Photography Awards, GDT European Wildlife Photographer of the Year, Outdoor Photographer of the Year and Bird Photographer of the Year, and more recently in the International Garden Photographer of the Year and UK Landscape Photographer of the Year competitions.

The Puffin Book
Published in Great Britain in 2021
by Graffeg Limited.

Written by Drew Buckley copyright © 2021.
Photography by Drew Buckley copyright ©
2021.

Designed and produced by Graffeg Limited
copyright © 2021.

Graffeg Limited, 24 Stradey Park Business
Centre, Mwrwg Road, Llangennech, Llanelli,
Carmarthenshire, SA14 8YP, Wales, UK.
Tel: 01554 824000. www.graffeg.com.

Drew Buckley is hereby identified as the
author of this work in accordance with
section 77 of the Copyrights, Designs and
Patents Act 1988.

A CIP Catalogue record for this book is
available from the British Library.

The publisher acknowledges the financial
support of the Books Council of Wales.
www.gwales.com.

ISBN 9781912654796

eBook ISBN 9781913634940

1 2 3 4 5 6 7 8 9

Photo credits

Cover and pages 2-141, 156, 158: Drew Buckley.

Page 142: Kate Wyatt.
www.katewyattartist.co.uk.

Page 145: John James Auburon.

Page 147: von Wright brothers.

Page 148: Aspire. www.aspireartwork.com.
Instagram: @aspireartwork.

Page 150: Faroe Islands postage stamp.

Page 151: Blue House.

Page 152: Puffin Mural, Seward, Alaska.
Amanda, 2018.

Page 155: Tufted puffins sculpture, Cannon
Beach, Oregon. Chris, 2013.

Endpapers: Linocuts by Jane Russ.

Books in the series

The Hare Book

The Fox Book

The Owl Book

The Red Squirrel Book

The Bee Book

The Robin Book

The Hedgehog Book

The Badger Book

The Puffin Book

www.graffeg.com